I AM . . .
The God That Healeth Thee

Exodus 15:26

To Mom on
Mothers Day
Love, David &
Lynda
2021

ISBN: 978-1-948362-51-1

Published by Whispering Pines Publishers, Shoals, Indiana

Printed by Country Pines, Inc., Shoals, Indiana

Printed in the United States of America

Contents

Acknowledgments

First and Foremost, I thank God for his instruction, direction and leading to complete this journal. I thank Him for the women of faith that He has placed in my life; for the amazing leaders that I have had the privilege to serve under and the gifts that He has place within me

To each one who believed, prayed, and spoke encouraging words over me during this long journey. Thank you, May God grant you double.

Cheryl Eagan, Cindy Smale, Debbie Hall, Wanda Wever, Kathy Sanders, Ruth Ann Hill and Rhonda Dyer. Thank you for loving me. May your cups be full and running over, may the beauty of the Lord be upon you, His grace surround you and His strength fill you.

Cheryl Mitchell; Thank you for creating the layout and design of this journal. May the Lord give increase more and more!

Debbie Hall: Thank you for taking the time to edit this journal. There is more to come.

Introduction: Saved to the Uttermost

The Amplified version of the verse from Hebrews 7:25 says "Therefore He is able also to save to the uttermost (completely, perfectly, finally, and for all time and eternity) those who come to God through Him, since He is always living to make petition to God and intercede with Him and intervene for them".

In its original Greek translation uttermost is the word Sozo which means to save, keep safe and sound, to rescue from danger or destruction, to save one (from injury or peril), to save a suffering one (from perishing), i.e. one suffering from disease. This is further described as to make well, heal, restore to health, to preserve one who is in danger of destruction, to save or rescue. The word denotes an all-encompassing healing, soul and spirit, of both present and future forgiveness from sin!

This is God's desire for you! His thoughts toward you are for good and not evil. He wishes, above all things that you would prosper and be in good health, just as your soul prospers. (3 John 1:2)

We are created as three part beings, body, soul, and spirit (1 Thessalonians 5:23). Our physical body and soul (mind, will and emotions), can all be affected by the doors that we open through disobedience to God's word, more commonly known as sin.

God sent his only son to this Earth so that we could be saved to the uttermost. He willingly laid down his life to make a way for us to live eternally, paying the price so we can be healed, restored and delivered from danger, destruction and eternal suffering! His mercy toward you is great! His faithfulness is everlasting and his compassion never fails.

There is no other name under Heaven by which men can be saved (Acts 4:7).

Barriers to Healing

Our sin, the sins of our parents, grandparents, and those before them all have an effect on our walk, struggles, victories, healing and freedom in Christ. Sin is an open door for our adversary, the devil, to come through. Whether it has been years, months, or days, doors which have been opened through disobedience to God's Word and active sin in our life give satan access and legal ground to work! Freedom comes through confession, repentance and receiving forgiveness that only Jehovah can provide.

Healing and spiritual growth can be blocked, stopped, or stunted. As you read through the list on the page that follows, keep a record of the areas the Lord brings to your attention Work though each one with confession and repentance Pray for the Lord to cleanse this area of your life and put it under the blood of Jesus. Thank God for the provision of his son on the Cross and what He has done in your life (Psalm 136).

The following pages may need to be revisited as you work your way through the 21 days of this healing journal.

Doubt and Unbelief:

- Unbelief kept Jesus from doing might works. Mark 6:4-6

- Doubt causes us to walk away from God. Heb 3:12

- Bitterness/Anger/Resentment:

- Bitter roots cause trouble and defile many. Heb 12:15

Fear:

Fear paralyzes us. It stops us from moving forward. There are many kinds of fear - fear of the unknown, fear of failure, fear of rejection, fear of man.

- Do not be afraid. Deut 31:6
- You have not received a spirit of fear. Rom 8: 15
- God did not give you a spirit of fear. 2 Tim 1:7
- Unconfessed Sin Blocks God from hearing us. Ps 66:18
- Separates from God. Isa 59:1, 2
- Worshiping other gods. Ex 20:4, 5

Continuing in Sin:

- Go and sin no more. Jn 8:11
- Repent, and turn from all your transgressions, so that iniquity will not be your ruin. Ezek 18:30
- Cease to do evil. Isa 1:16

Occult involvement:

Occult means hidden. Satan loves to work in the hidden areas of our life, in the dark. He will go to great lengths to bury things from your past to keep you bound and the doorways open so he can have access to your life. It takes the light of Jehovah to shine into the secret places and expose those things that need to be dealt with.

- Come out and be separate. 2 Cor 6:17
- Do not turn to mediums or familiar spirits. Lev 20:6, 19:31
- Sorcerers. Rev 21:8
- Rebellion is as witchcraft. 1 Sam 15:23
- We are to submit to God, and resist the devil. James 4:

Salvation

"And there is salvation in no one else; for there is no other name under heaven that has been given among men by which we must be saved." Act 4:12 NASV

Confess:

If we confess our sins, He is faithful and just to forgive us our sins and to cleanse us from all unrighteousness- 1 John 1:9 1

Repent:

If my people who are called by My name will humble themselves, and pray and seek My face, and turn from their wicked ways, then I will hear from heaven, and will forgive their sin and heal their land.2 Chron. 7:14

Those whom I love I rebuke and discipline. So be earnest and repent - Rev 3:19

Then God saw their works that they turned from their evil way; and God relented from the disaster that He had said He would bring upon them, and He did not do it - Jonah 3:10

Receive:

But as many as received Him, to them He gave the right to become children of God, to those who believed in His name – John 1:12

I am coming soon. Hold on to what you have, so that no one will take your crown. The one who is victorious I will make a pillar in the temple of my God. Never again will they leave it. I will write on them the name of my God and the name of the city of my God, the new Jerusalem, which is coming down out of heaven from my God; and I will also write on them my new name. Whoever has ears, let them hear what the Spirit says to the churches - Rev 3:11-13

Take your time as you work through each day of this journal, even though it has 21 days. If you need more than one day for God to work in a certain area of your life, allow the Holy Spirt to complete the work He desires to complete. Some of our hurts are deep and have been there a long time. The Lord knows how much healing or deliverance we need for the moment. Trust him to work all things together for your good! My hope is that you finish with healing and a new strength of God, that peace be in your borders and your walls become walls of salvation!

May you be saved to the uttermost!

My Prayer for You

My prayer for each of you, as you study and meditate through the pages of this journal, is that you find what you have need of. That God meets with you on new levels! That you reach higher heights and deeper depths in The Lord! That all deception of the devil is removed from you and that you find understanding, hope and healing through the words of The Lord. My desire is the desire of the Lord for you, that you choose life and life more abundantly - John 10:10.

Day 1 – Salvation is From the Lord

Jonah 2:9 (NASB)

> But I will sacrifice to you with the voice of thanksgiving that which I have vowed, I will say salvation is from the Lord

Part of our heritage as children of the Lord are the benefits and blessings that David describes in Psalm 103, verses two through four: "Bless the Lord, Oh my soul, and forget not all His benefits; Who forgives all your iniquity, Who heals all your diseases, Who redeems your life from destruction, Who crowns you with loving kindness and tender mercies".

It is God's desire for all His children to experience the fullness of His salvation, redemption, and healing. As His sons and daughters, we have been given authority to stand against our adversary and to walk in victory over every plan that he forms against us.

Merriam-Webster defines "salvation" as deliverance from the power and effects of sin, preservation or deliverance from harm, ruin, or loss.

As we yield our life to the plan that God has prepared for us, seek His truth and follow His word, we will find freedom from the power of sin and death. We will also be free from the effect that sin could have upon our life and the generations that follow after us.

Something inside Jonah caused him to believe that he could run from the presence of The Lord. That decision led to his three-day

15

journey in the belly of a whale. Scripture tells us that the seaweed entangled him, and the waves passed over him. That experience left him willing to obey God and surrender every doubt and fear to His call.

Jonah didn't know how long he would be in this place of affliction; he wasn't sure if he would live or die. He did know that it was his disobedience to the Lord that led him to this dark and lonely pit. It was from this place that Jonah called out to God with the words from today's scripture,

"Salvation is from the Lord".

The Hebrew word for salvation in the scripture from Jonah 2:9 is Yeshua. A common name for God in Jonah's day, Yeshua means deliverance, prosperity, or victory.

The suffering and struggles of our life may come through unexpected life experiences, the death of a loved one, a major change in our life, or a serious illness. They may come through a choice that we have made or by the hand of our adversary. In every situation, God desires to be our salvation. He wants to preserve us from harm, ruin or loss and bring us the victory that only He can bring.

As we acknowledge who God is, ask forgiveness for our disobedience and Praise Him in our storm, He will move in our life, just as He did in the life of Jonah.

The benefits that David wrote about in Psalm 103 are for every believer. If you have never asked God into your heart, there is no better time than now. God has a plan for you that is greater than anything you could design on your own. He is waiting for His children to come to Him. If today is your day for salvation, pray the following prayer with me:

Yeshua, I want you to be the God of my heart. I confess the sins of my past and ask you to forgive me. Thank you for loving me and sending your son, Jesus, to pay the price for my salvation upon the cross of Calvary. Amen

Healing Prayer

Thank you for pulling me from the deep and lonely places where the billows tried to overtake me. Thank you for every victory in my life. The ones I can see and the ones I cannot see. Amen.

Healing Confession

"Behold, God is my salvation, I will trust and not be afraid; For the Lord God is my strength and song and He has become my salvation." Isaiah 12:2 NASB

Healing Action

1. Pray for the Lord to begin to reveal Himself to you as your deliverer, healer, and savior!

2. There are many examples of God's salvation woven throughout this Journal. As you work through the next 20 days, pray for the Lord to help you see His salvation (deliverance, perseverance, healing, and victory) in your life.

God's Word for Us

And there is Salvation in no one else for there is no other name under heaven given among men by which we must be saved." — Acts 4:12 ESV

But I have trusted in your steadfast love; my heart shall rejoice in your salvation. — Psalm 13:5 ESV

But I am afflicted and in pain; Let your salvation, O God, set me up on high. — Psalm 69:29 ESV

For I am not ashamed of the gospel of Christ, for it is the power of God to salvation. For everyone who believes, for the Jew first and for the Greek. — Romans 1:16 NKJV

Oh come; let us sing to the Lord! Let us shout joyfully to the Rock of our salvation. — Psalm 95:1 NKJV

For God alone my soul waits in silence; From Him comes my salvation He alone is my rock and my salvation; my fortress; I shall not be greatly shaken. — Psalm 62:1, 2 NKJV

My Thoughts Today

_____

_____

_____

_____

_____

_____

_____

_____

_____

_____

_____

_____

_____

_____

_____

_____

_____

Day 2 – Abundant Life

John 10:10 (ESV)

> The thief comes only, to steal, and kill, and destroy: I am come that they might have life and have it more abundantly.

We have an adversary who takes every opportunity available to work against us as we press forward in the Kingdom of God. He is watching and studying the choices we make, the weak areas of our life and the sins of the generations who have gone before us. His attempts to destroy us, discredit God and stop us from moving forward in the Lord never cease. For every plan that our adversary devises to steal kill and destroy, God has a plan for victory, one that includes us having a hope and a future in him (Jeremiah 29:11).

Peter and the other disciples did not expect to see Jesus the morning He called out to them from the shore of the Sea of Galilee. (John 21: 4-12). Only a few days earlier, the men had visited the empty tomb and watched as Thomas touched Jesus nail-pierced hands.

After a long night of fishing on the sea, the disciples could only respond "No" to Jesus' question, "Do you have anything to eat?" Perhaps their willingness to follow the instructions of a stranger and cast their nets back out on the other side of the boat came because there was something familiar about Him.

As the men pulled their abundantly-filled nets out of the water,

God opened their understanding, and they knew that they were speaking with Jesus, their beloved friend who they believed they would never see again.

The Greek definition for abundantly from John 10:10 means exceeding some number, measure, or rank, over and above, more than necessary, extraordinary, surpassing, or uncommon.

Perhaps Jesus made this third appearance to the disciples to remind them that they could never return to their old life. Maybe He wanted them to know, if they continued to follow His will, they would always have more than enough.

Everything Jesus did had a purpose, something to teach, deliver or impart. It wasn't uncommon for Him to use a physical illustration to teach a spiritual principle. I believe this day on the shore of Galilee was no different. After filling the disciples' nets with more than enough, Jesus reminded them to feed His sheep.

There are times in our life when it is hard to remember that God desires to supply us with more than enough. The issues of life crowd in on us just as they did the disciples that night on the small boat. The men were tired and hungry; all their efforts had failed; and they did not recognize the voice of Jesus. Yet, as the men obeyed and cast their nets back out into the water, they were filled with more than enough.

The peace, healing, and freedom that God has for your life is over and above anything you could imagine. Perhaps you think that you are not worthy of His affection or that He has forgotten about you.

Maybe you have been crying out to Him for a specific need. Do not give up! Let go of every limitation and reservation. Cast your net back out into the water one more time and see what the Lord will do. Trust Him. Give Him one more opportunity to fill the empty place within you, to break the chains that have bound you and to heal your deepest wound. Our God is well able!

Healing Prayer

Father, thank you for doing more than I could ask, think, or hope for. Help me to understand your deepest desire for my life. Teach me how to walk in the abundant supply that you have planned for me. Amen

Healing Confession

My hope will not be cut off in Jesus' name. Proverbs 23:18
I will walk in the fullness of Your plan for my life. John 1:16

Healing Action

1. Ask the Lord to reveal any areas of your life that need healing. Make a list in the space below.
2. Thank God for healing these places.
3. Ask the Lord to show you any areas of unbelief in your life. Make a list in the space below.
4. Confess each area to the Lord. Ask Him to forgive you for holding onto unbelief and not trusting Him more.
5. Ask the Lord to fill you with a greater measure of faith (unbelief works to steal our faith).
6. Record any declarations of faith you want to stand on over the next 21 days.

God's Word for Us

"The Lord is my strength and my song, and He has become my salvation; He is my God, and I will Praise Him, my father's God, and I will exalt Him." — Exodus 15:2 ESV

Behold I will bring it health and healing; I will heal them and reveal to them the abundance of peace and truth. — Jeremiah 33:6 NKJV

Now to him, who is able to do far more abundantly than all that we ask or think, according to the power at work within us. — Ephesians 3:20 ESV

The Lord will open to you His good treasure, the heavens, to give the rain to your land in its season, and to bless all the work of your hand. You shall lend to many nations, but you shall not borrow. — Deuteronomy28:12 NKJV

May the Lord give you increase, you and your children. — Psalm 115:14 ESV

Today's Thoughts

_____

_____

_____

_____

_____

_____

_____

_____

_____

_____

_____

_____

_____

_____

_____

Day 3 – Faith for Healing

Mark 5:25 -34

> And he said to her, "Daughter, your faith has made you well. Go in peace and be healed of your affliction."

Faith will carry us through every fiery trial, it will demolish fear and allow us to see God's desire for our life come to pass. Our faith is called into action the moment we surrender our life to Christ. From this time forward faith is a journey, something that grows within us as we go deeper in the Lord

The woman, who was known for her issue of blood in the fifth chapter of Mark, had endured many struggles until the day she pressed her way through the crowd. Everything that kept her discouraged and disappointed was forgotten as she reached out to touch the hem of Jesus' garment.

Something had driven this woman past the loss of her health, finances, and family. After twelve years, of unsuccessful doctor visits, mental, emotional and physical weariness, she found the healing that she had waited so long to see.

The purity law of the day required women with vaginal bleeding to separate themselves from everyone. These women were not to cook, clean, or serve meals. Because they were viewed as unclean according to the law, anyone or anything they touched was unclean (Lev 15:19).

On top of every other struggle this woman had to endure, she was left alone, isolated from those she loved and without the physical and emotional support that many of us rely on to get through the tough times of life. Every doubt must have come alive with hope as the woman with the issue of blood heard the news of Jesus, the man from Nazareth who was traveling the countryside, healing the sick, delivering the oppressed and giving sight to the blind.

As the crowd pressed closer to Jesus, so did this woman who was about to be known for her faith. Forgetting about the tradition of her day, leaving behind doubt, unbelief, and the judgment of others, she made her way through the crowd. Knowing the risk of touching everyone, she passed, she chose to follow the voice of faith within her. The words that she spoke just minutes before. "If only I could touch the hem of His garment, I know I will be made whole", suddenly became a reality. Her faith led her, her belief carried her and Jesus healed her.

Scripture tells us that God gives each of us a measure of faith. (Romans 12:3 NKJV). We can take the measure, of faith that we have been given and hide it just as the man in the parable of the talents did (Matt. 25:18), or we can use our measure; walk in it, speak it and live it, and watch it become something much greater. (Matt. 5:20).

There are many stories of faith in the Bible of people who received their healing because they believed and those who received their healing on the faith of others. It is important in this walk with the Lord to surround ourselves with faith-filled friends -- those who can speak into our life, stand with us in prayer and support us in our time of need.

Perhaps you are just beginning your faith journey, maybe you have walked by faith for many years. Wherever you are, God is calling each of us to a deeper level. He is looking for those who are willing to step out and walk in His miraculous, unwavering faith.

Healing Prayer

Father, increase my faith today. Help me to speak Your words over my circumstances and the circumstances of those around me. I surrender all my (fill in the blank, fear, doubt. Etc.) _____, to You. Amen.

Healing Confession

I believe in Your healing power...................Jeremiah 17:14
You reward me when I seek You...................Hebrews 11:6
By Your stripes, I am healed.............................. Isaiah 53:5

Healing Action

Faith requires an action. The woman with the issue of blood pressed through the crowd around her. She left the familiar place she had been in and stepped out into the unknown.

Pray for the Lord to give you a scripture or action that you need to take to activate your faith. In the Bible, Jesus always gave what was asked for in faith. Record what the Lord gives you in the space below.

God's Word for Us

Heal me, Oh Lord, and I shall be healed; save me, and I shall be saved. For You are my praise. — Jeremiah 17: 14 ESV

For whatever is born of God overcomes the world. And this is the victory that has overcome the world, our faith. — 1 John 5 :4 NKJV

But without faith it is impossible to please Him, for he who comes to God must believe that He is, and that He is a rewarder of those who diligently seek Him. — Hebrews 11:6 NKJV

So Jesus said to them, "Because of your unbelief; for assuredly, I say to you, if you have faith as a mustard seed, you will say to this mountain 'move from here to there', and it will move; and nothing will be impossible for you. — Matthew 17:20 NKJV

For we walk by faith and not by sight. — 2 Corinthians 5:7 ESV

Watch, stand fast in the faith, be brave, be strong. Let all that you do be done with love. — 1 Corinthians 16:13 NKJV

My Thoughts Today

_____

_____

_____

_____

_____

_____

_____

_____

_____

_____

_____

_____

_____

_____

_____

_____

_____

Day 4 – The Heart of the Matter

Proverbs 4:23 (AMP)

> Watch over your heart with all diligence for from it flow the springs of life

The heart is a fairly small organ in comparison to all of its capabilities. When functioning as it was created, this vessel processes every drop of blood as it circulates throughout the human body. From the time of conception until the time of death, its beat is continuous, providing our main source of life. It also functions as a seating place for our innermost character, emotions, courage, and appetites (as in what we desire, love, and crave). Everything we are is connected to this vital organ.

Few things are as sweet to the soul as a cold drink from a clear mountain spring on a hot summer day. From the moment the water passes our lips until it settles into the tissues and organs of our body, every drop is refreshing and satisfying.

What would happen if that same mountain spring became contaminated? It is a hot summer day, you are tired and thirsty, your muscles are craving a fresh filling. You take a drink only to find what you expected to be refreshing and satisfying has become undrinkable.

Matthew 13:25 speaks of an enemy who creeps in and sows' tares among the wheat while the men slept. Friends, our adversary who loves to work when we are not watchful will use any circumstance of our life to sow tares of bitterness, unforgiveness or resentment into our heart. The longer these tares remain in our life, the greater their influence will have over us eventually affecting our ability to see our circumstances clearly, trust others and overcome the troubles we face.

After three days in the wilderness, Moses led the Israelites to Marah the place of bitter water (Exodus 15). It did not take long for the people to complain to Moses, allowing the bitterness of their own heart to seep out. The Israelites had learned to expect the worst as slaves in Egypt. This day at Marah must have seemed no different to them.

The bitterness that remained in the hearts of the Israelites from their time in captivity came out time and time again during their journey in the wilderness. It kept them from seeing the miracles of God and ultimately from entering the land of God's promise.

Part of the Greek definition for spring in Proverbs 4 means source (of life). Our Heart is the source of who we are; of what we think, feel, and believe. It is the source of our courage, fear, and disappointment. Is it any wonder that we are instructed in God's Word to guard this precious vessel above everything?

Perhaps God wanted the Israelites to realize something bigger than they grasped that day at Marah. Maybe He wanted them to see that what was in their heart was just as bitter as the water they were unable to drink. Possibly, He wanted them to know that He could take the bitterness of their past, the pain of their slavery, and the sorrow of their spirit and turn it into something sweeter and better than they had ever known.

We cannot walk through this world unscathed by pain or hurt. We can be diligent to pull up the weeds our adversary tries to sow in our heart quickly, surrender them to God and keep our heart clean.

Healing Prayer

Father, heal the hurt and pain of my past. Remove any hidden seeds that have been sown in my heart while I was unaware. I surrender them to you. I pray for the springs of my heart to become clean and pure! Set Your guard over my heart, Father, and help me to watch diligently over it in days to come. Amen.

Healing Confession

I set my heart on You, O Lord............................ Psalm 57:7

I trust in You with my whole heart .... Proverbs 3:5

You make my heart steadfast, O Lord............... Psalm 57:7

Healing Action

1. Pray for the Lord to show you anything in your heart that needs to be removed or healed. Make a list in the space below as He reveals them to you

2. Surrender each issue to the Lord, asking Him to forgive you for allowing them to have a place in your life.

3. Thank God for His grace and mercy in your life. The Israelites could not see how God moved on their behalf as they journeyed through the wilderness. They had set their focus on what they did not have instead of the miracles in front of them. A thankful heart

is important in our journey with the Lord. It keeps our focus on Him and all that He is doing and removes the opportunity for our adversary to pull us into a deeper pit of despair, regret, and discouragement.

4. Make a list of 5 to 10 things that you are thankful for in the space below.

God's Word for Us

Trust in the Lord with all your heart and lean not on your own understanding; in all your ways acknowledge Him, and shall direct your paths. — Proverbs 3:5, 6 NKJV

And you will seek Me and find Me when you search for Me all your heart. — Jeremiah 29; 13 NKLV

Create in me a clean heart, O God, and renew a right spirit within me. — Psalms 51: 10 KJV

You shall love the Lord your God with all your heart, with all your soul, and with all your strength. — Deuteronomy 6:5 NKJV

For where your treasure is, there your heart will be also. — Mathew 6:21 ESV

My son, give Me your heart, and let your eyes observe My ways — Proverbs 23:36 ESV

My Thoughts Today

Day 5 - Forgiveness from the Heart

Matthew 18:21

> Jesus said to him, "I do not say to you up to seventy times, but up to seventy times seven.

True freedom comes through our submission to God and His Word. As we surrender the areas of our life that limit and bind us from becoming who God has called us to be, we make room for more of His peace, power, and anointing. His character can begin to blossom within us, His spirit will fill us in greater measure, and we will become a living testimony to those around us.

Becoming a disciple of Jesus Christ means that our rights are now those of the Kingdom of God. It is our right to love one another (John 13: 34, 35); to pray for those who persecute us (Matthew 5:44), and to forgive those who sin against us (Luke 11:4).

Jesus used the parable of the unmerciful servant to illustrate His answer to Peter's question "How many times shall my brother sin against me and I forgive him? Up to seven times?" The number seven represents completeness in the word of God. Yet here, we learn that Peter's idea of forgiving others seven times, cannot compare with Jesus' instructions to forgive others seventy times seven.

The seventy times seven forgiveness that Jesus taught about goes beyond anything that we are capable of in our own ability. It requires the character of Christ within us and the power of the Holy Spirit working though us.

The unforgiving servant in Matthew 18 had no mercy or compassion. His unwillingness to forgive a much smaller debt than he was forgiven, along with his decision to place his servant in jail delivered him to a place of torture. His debt that had once been forgiven was reversed, his freedom was lost, and his family would never be the same.

The Greek word for torture in Matthew 18:34 means to be harassed, distressed, tortured, or tormented; to be questioned by applying torture, to vex with grievous pains of body or mind. This word also speaks of those at sea who are struggling with a headwind.

Refusing to forgive those who have wronged or hurt us, allowing our heart to become hardened against them or embracing bitterness, resentment or offense will all play a part in our own imprisonment. Our sentence may vary according to the length and degree that we hold onto any harmful or destructive emotion.

Forgiving others, may not be easy. Releasing them from the offence, bitterness or resentment that surround our unforgiveness can be even harder.

As we forgive those who have wronged or hurt us, prison doors will open. The distress, torment, or torture that have been working against us will leave. Headwinds will cease and we will have a greater measure of God's peace.

Healing Prayer

Father open my eyes to any unforgiveness that has hidden itself away in the corner of my heart. Forgive me, as I forgive others. Help me pray for my enemies (Luke 6:27). Bless those who curse me and love those who despitefully use me. In Jesus' name I pray. Amen

Healing Confession

Let the words of my mouth and the meditation of my heart be acceptable in Your sight, O Lord, my strength, and my Redeemer. Psalm 19:14

Healing Action

1. Pray for the Lord to show you anyone that you need to forgive, (including yourself and God) Make a list in the space below
2. Confess any unforgiveness to The Lord
3. Repent and ask the Lord to forgive you for being a vessel of unforgiveness.

Look at the following list. Mark any issues you have been dealing with and ask the Holy Spirit to show you if they are attached to any unforgiveness in your life

*   Harassment (to irritate or torment)
*   Distress (hurt, suffering, anguish, anxiety, pain);

41

- Feelings of being tortured or tormented (can be mentally or emotionally)
- Struggling with a headwind (can't seem to make progress, even with simple tasks of getting ready for work or completing housework you seem to take one step forward and two back)
- Agitated or irritated (this often comes for no apparent reason)
- Feeling annoyed (for no apparent reason)
- Feelings being tossed about (mentally or emotionally)
- Vexation (annoy, distress, agitate, shake up) – vexation often feels like an emotional raw wound that someone is rubbing, causing an irritation.

God's Word for Us

If we confess our sins, He is faithful and just to forgive us our sins, and to cleanse us from all unrighteousness. — 1 John 1:9 ESV

So, if the Son sets you free, you will be free indeed. — John 8:36 ESV

And whenever you stand praying, forgive if you have anything against anyone, so that your Father also who is in heaven may forgive you your trespasses. — Mark 11:25 ESV

I acknowledged my sin to You, and my iniquity I have not hidden. I said, "I will confess my transgressions to the Lord," and You forgave the iniquity of my sin. — Psalm 32: 5 NKJV

For if you forgive men their trespasses, your heavenly Father will also forgive you; but if ye forgive not men their trespasses, neither will your Father forgive your trespasses". — Matthew 6: 14,15 NKJV

My Thoughts Today

Day 6 – Trading My Sorrows

John 16:20b

> Your sorrow shall be turned into joy

King David walked through many seasons of rejection and loneliness. He understood the Joy of the Lord and the deep sorrow of this world. David penned one of his prayers about sorrow in Psalm 13 NKJV

"How long, O Lord? Will you forget me forever? How long will You hide Your face from me? How long shall I take counsel in my soul, Having sorrow in my heart daily? How long will my enemy be exalted over me? Consider and hear me, O Lord, my God".

Sorrow comes to steal our joy and smother us with disappointment. Deep sorrow comes with a breaking and sadness incomparable to much else. It settles in the core of who we are and changes our ability to see the good in everyday life. Deep sorrow leaves us feeling alone and numb, with thoughts of being on the outside, watching everyone else live as life passes us by.

Merriam-Webster describes sorrow as distress, sadness, or regret, especially for the loss of someone loved. Sorrow can be the cause of grief, sadness, heartache, or heartbreak. It can come with a deep feeling of distress caused by loss, disappointment or other misfortune in our lives.

Jesus was despised and rejected by men. He was a man of sorrows, acquainted with grief (Isaiah 53:5). He knew what it felt like to experience pain, He understood the sorrow of loneliness and how it felt when those around Him failed to understand His thoughts and actions. Yes, He was the son of God; but while He was here on earth, Jesus experienced pain, sorrow and loneliness just like us. He overcame everything at the cross so we could overcome the experiences of our own life.

David completed Psalm 13 with the following words: I have trusted in Your mercy; my heart shall rejoice in Your salvation. I will sing to the Lord, Because He has dealt bountifully with me".

Times of sorrow leave us asking the same questions as David ask in Psalm 13. Sorrow's ultimate plan is to steal or stifle the Joy of the Lord within us. Nehemiah 8:10 tells us that the Joy of the lord is our strength. David worked through his place of sorrow, He pressed through every question and chose to offer praise to the God that he knew so well.

Deep sorrow has visited my life several times. Standing at the door of my heart, waiting like a wet blanket to smother out the fire and passion of God, working to destroy my peace and steal my joy. Sorrow has come through circumstances with people, through disappointments of life and, at times, through the loss of someone I loved. It found its way into my life through people who did not know they were being used and through those ready and willing to partner with it. It used people

46

who believed they knew what needed to be said but lacked the love and wisdom to deliver their words without causing further pain.

I asked the Lord why my seasons of sorrow came so often and lasted so long. Piece by piece, He has given me understanding, healed my heart and set me free. God has taught me that I can stand against every plan of my adversary and overcome all things through Him. He has filled my life with hope, and the knowledge that no matter what I am going through, He is with me and He will never leave me or forsake me.

God brought David out of his time of sorrow. He rescued me, and He will do the same for you. Brothers and Sisters in Christ, God does not send this deep sorrow or the thoughts of loneliness that come with it.

Today, I know that we must stand against the thoughts which come to destroy us. Study the Word of God and use that word against every scheme of our adversary. We must not stop launching our arrows and wielding the Word of God until we know that our victory is complete.

Healing Prayer

Father, send Your healing power into my life today. Break the bars which have held me in places of deep sorrow, loneliness, and heartache. Awaken my spirit from numbness and cause the rivers of sorrow over my life to become fountains of joy. In Jesus' name, Amen.

Healing Confession

Jehovah is my healer and deliverer; through Him I am free from the pit of the dark sorrow Exodus 15:26
God will turn my sorrow into joy. John 16:20

Healing Action

Choose a scripture from today's scripture page and speak it out loud over yourself at least three times throughout the day. Make the scripture personal, (Example: Isaiah 41:10, I will not be dismayed, You are my God, You will strengthen me, You will uphold me with Your righteous right hand).

God's Word for Us

And the ransomed of the Lord shall return and come to Zion with singing, everlasting joy shall be upon their heads; they shall obtain gladness and joy, and sorrow and sighing shall flee away. — Isaiah 51:11 ESV

For his anger is but for a moment, His favor is for life; Weeping may endure for a night, but joy comes in the morning — Psalm 30:5 NKJV

You have turned my mourning into dancing: You have loosed my sackcloth and clothed me with gladness. —Psalm 30:11 ESV

These things I have spoken to you, that My Joy may be in you and that your joy may be full. — John 15:11 NKJV

Restore to me the joy of Your salvation and uphold me by Your generous Spirit — Psalm 51:12 NKJV

The Lord gives strength to His people, the Lord blesses His people with peace — Psalm 29:11 NKJV

My Thoughts Today

_____

_____

_____

_____

_____

_____

_____

_____

_____

_____

_____

_____

_____

_____

_____

_____

_____

Day 7 - The Lord is Near to the Broken-Hearted

Psalms 34:18

> The Lord is near to the broken hearted and saves those who are crushed in spirit.

Jeremiah records the story of a potter and the piece of clay that became marred in his hands as he formed it on his potter's wheel (Jeremiah 18). The potter took the marred clay broke it and began to remake it into a new vessel -- one that he believed would be of greater value and a better reflection of himself.

The beauty in becoming a child of God is that once we have given our heart to Him, we are never out of His hands. It is here, from this place of safety, that God will protect us from all that was meant to corrupt, ruin, or harm us. It is also here, in the hands of the Master Potter where we can be molded into a vessel of splendor and of far greater worth.

Jesus and the disciples were gathered around the table at the house of Simon the Leper when a woman entered the room with a flask of costly oil. (Matthew 26). Looking past the tradition of her day and all who were gathered in the house, the unnamed woman made her way over to Jesus. She broke open the flask and began to pour its costly contents over Him. As the aroma of the oil filled the air, indignation flooded the hearts of some of the men who were in the room.

When those who were offended began to reason among themselves that the oil could have been sold and the money used to help the poor, Jesus silenced their words.

I cannot help but think that the real question in the heart of these men might have been. Who do you think you are and what right do you have to come in here and interrupt us? Can't you see that we are breaking bread with the Master?

Merriam Webster defines indignation as an anger aroused by something unjust or unworthy. Perhaps the fact that this woman was bold enough to interrupt these men who counted themselves special caused them to become indignant towrd her. Maybe it was because she seemed to understand something they could not. Whatever the reason, Jesus put all of their negative words and thoughts to rest as he spoke "Why do you trouble her?

She has done a good work for me and wherever this gospel is preached in the whole world, what this woman has done will be told as a memorial to her". (Matthew 26: 13)

In Jesus day it was customary for a woman to keep an alabaster flask full of costly oil as part of a dowry. On her wedding night, the wife would break open the flask and pour its contents over the feet of her husband symbolizing her love, submission, and devotion to him.

The unnamed woman, whose actions angered those around her,

held nothing back in her worship as she poured the oil over Jesus to prepare Him for what was to come. She allowed those in the room to see her love, submission, and devotion to One who was so worthy.

The Hebrew word for broken in Psalm 34:18 means to break down, crush, to be broken or shattered. It also means to break out or bring to birth.

Dear friends, the things of this life that have been used against you, the situations that have tried to crush, break or shatter you, are the very things that God will use to break you out -- out of your current situation, out of the indignation and judgment of others, out of the old and into the new.

Healing Prayer

Thank you, Father, for making the broken places of my life into something new Thank You for keeping me in the safety of Your hands, where no plan of the enemy can prosper against me. May my life become a sweet-smelling aroma in Your kingdom.

Healing Confession

The Lord is my strength and my shield; my heart trusts in Him and I am helped (Psalm 28:7 NASV).
My God will save me out of all my distresses. Psalms 107:19 NASV

Healing Action

1. Pray for the Lord to reveal to you if there is anyone you need to forgive, who may have knowingly or unknowingly been vessels of breaking, bruising or crushing in your life. Pour out your forgiveness on them.
2. Allow God to pour His healing oil over your wounds, refreshing and restoring you in a greater measure.

God's Word for Us

The Lord is near to the broken-hearted and saves the crushed in spirit. — Psalm 34:18 ESV

The sacrifices of God are a broken spirit: a broken and a contrite heart, these, O God, You will not despise. — Psalm 51:17 NKJV

He heals the broken-hearted and binds up their wounds. — Psalm 147:3 NKJV

He sent His Word and healed them and delivered them from their destructions. — Psalm 107:20 ESV

Heal me, O Lord, and I shall be healed; Save me, and I shall be saved, for You are my praise. — Jeremiah 17:14 ESV

Behold, I will bring to it health and healing; I will heal them and reveal to them the abundance of peace and truth. — Jeremiah 33:6 ESV

My Thoughts Today

Day 8 - All Things New

2 Corinthians 5:17

> Therefore, if anyone is in Christ, he is a new creation; old things have passed away; behold, all things have become new.

Becoming a new creature in Christ is not something that happens suddenly. For most, it is a process that we must walk out and allow God to create within us. Our transformation can be long and laborious. It can require us to endure trial by fire, and perseverance,

In the early days of my own pursuit for God, I found myself frequently asking Him to take the old nature that I had been born with and walked in for so long and make it into the new nature that I read about in His Word. I was looking for an almost instant change - a sudden moment which would take what I believed to be undesirable within me and make it into something that I believed was more desirable. It took years for me to understand that if God had granted my request, I would not have become His vessel; one that had developed through affliction, trial, and error. A vessel that had more of His Spirit, love and wisdom.

At times, my request for change came from a desire to be more like Jesus. Other times, it was driven from my need to be loved and accepted by God and man. More often, my request to be changed came out of my weariness in dealing with the same issue over and over again.

I often found myself identifying with Paul when he said, "For I do not understand my own actions, for I do not do what I want, but I do the very thing I hate" (Romans 7:15 ESV). There were moments when I hated my reaction to the circumstances around me and even more moments when I hated myself. It was something that took years for me to understand and even longer to overcome.

Job described his own journey of transformation in the 19th verse of chapter 23; "but He knows the way that I take, when He has tried me, I shall come out as gold." We cannot serve God to our fullest if we remain the same as we were when we came to Him. Our walk must be one of transformation from the old self of flesh, to a new creature that is full of the love and power of the Holy Spirt.

Diamonds are one of the most luxurious and desired stones known to man. Before they reach their desired state, each diamond must be put through a stringent process includes fire, pressure, cutting and polishing.

As followers of Christ who desire to reach our full potential and become the radiant gem that we are created to be. We must also endure the pressures of our adversary. We must walk through trial by fire and have everything that does not resemble the Lord to be cut away from our life.

Eight represents new beginnings and coming full circle in the Bible. The word "become" in 2 Corinthians 5:17 means "to begin". This day can be a day of new beginning for you! As you let go of any doubt and fear of becoming who God has called you to be, surrender any guilt or shame of your past and embrace the truth of God's word, you will be empowered by His Spirit to move forward into your destiny.

Each step forward counts in the Kingdom of God. Every victory, whether large or small is a victory won. God has miracles to perform in you and He has miracles to perform through you.

As we are changed from our old nature into the new nature of Christ, we will lose interest in our old ways. What captured us will have to loosen its grip as we desire the new and better things that the Lord has prepared for us.

Healing Prayer

Thank you, Father for new beginnings. Thank you for being my strength when I am weak, for loving me when I feel unlovable and for not giving up on me, especially in those times that I wanted to give up on myself.

Healing Confession

I am crucified with Christ; nevertheless I live; yet not I, but Christ lives in me; and the life which I now live in the flesh I live by the faith of the Son of God, who loved me, and gave himself for me. Galatians 2:20

Healing Action

1. Pray for the Lord to reveal any areas of your old nature that have not been surrendered to him. Make a list in the space below.
2. Surrender the areas on your list above to the Lord.
3. Pray for the Lord to fill any void in your life with His Spirit.
4. Thank Him for moving you to a new level and for His faithfulness to your life.

God's Word for Us

But as it is written, eye hath not seen, nor ear heard, neither have entered into the heart of man, the things which God hath prepared for those that love him. — 1 Corinthians 2:9 NKJV

I have been crucified with Christ; it is no longer I who live, but Christ lives in me; and the life which I now live in the flesh I live by faith in the Son of God, who loved me and gave Himself for me. — Galatians 2:20 NKJV

For we are His workmanship, created in Christ Jesus for good works, which God prepared beforehand that we should walk in them. — Ephesians 2:10 NKJV

But we all, with unveiled face, beholding as in a mirror the glory of the Lord, are being transformed into the same image from glory to glory, just as by the Spirit of the Lord. — 2 Corinthians 3:18 NKJV

And to put on the new self, created after the likeness of God in true righteousness and holiness. — Ephesians 4:24 ESV

My Thoughts Today

_____

_____

_____

_____

_____

_____

_____

_____

_____

_____

_____

_____

_____

_____

_____

_____

_____

Day 9 – In Your Brokenness, You Can Shine

Philippians 1:6

> Being Confident of this very thing, that He who began a good work in you will complete it until the day of Jesus Christ
> Philippians 1:6

It can take years for the wounded and broken places of our life to be restored and made into something new. As we walk through this healing process, each reminder that God is at work, encourages us to hold on until we see the completion of His promise.

During the many years of our friendship Kathy and I have had the privilege of encouraging each other, praying together, and standing for the promises of God in our life. Each time we met, God was in our midst filling us with laughter, encouragement, and special moments. The day that Kathy came into my office carrying a large brown satchel in her hands was no different from many of the other times we have shared over the years.

Within minutes , I found myself holding the large brown satchel that Kathy brought with her. I listened closely to the story of what was about to become one of the most meaningful gifts I have ever received.

I am not sure if Kathy knew that the gift inside the satchel was one of many things that God would ask her to trade for her new life as a

63

missionary. I know this - the lamp that I received from this woman of faith will always serve as a reminder that God uses us in times and ways we cannot understand or imagine.

At first glance, I did not see that part of the glass globe, which once surrounded the lightbulb of the lamp had been broken. As I listened to Kathy and the journey of the light, I thought about God's mercy and grace, that His ways are not our ways and His thoughts are not our thoughts.

That morning, before Kathy came into my office, she placed the satchel with the lamp into her locker. As she returned that afternoon and opened the locker door, the satchel fell to the floor, breaking the pink flower-shaped globe that once surrounded the lamp's electric bulb.

Saddened by what happened. Kathy thought the lamp had lost its value and was no longer worth giving away. The Holy Spirit interrupted Kathy's plan and left her with these instructions. Give her the lamp and tell her "even in her brokenness, she can shine."

My friend did not know that I had spent many years struggling with rejection, shame, and regret. But God knew! He knew exactly what I needed that day. He also knew how to send a gift that would be a continual reminder to trust Him and His plan for my life.

I think about Gideon and his army who placed torches inside of clay pitchers (Judges, Chapter 7). When given the command, the army broke the pitchers and yelled "the sword of the Lord and Gideon". The lights that were hidden inside the pitchers became visible to the

Israelites and the army of Gideon received their victory.

There is a light of God that shines through us, and there is a light of God's Glory that will shine upon us. The more time we spend in the presence of the Lord, the greater His glory will become upon our life

The light of God's Glory, that could be seen on the face of Moses as he returned from Mount Sinai, caused the Israeli people to fear. It became the reason that Moses veiled his face as he spoke to the people. It was also a testimony that he had been in the presence of the lord.

Each time I look at the light that sits on a shelf in my family room, I remember the friend who traded all she had known for a life of prayer, travel, and ministry. I remember that God can use us when we are broken, wounded or weary. Most of all, I remember the truth that God can shine more brightly through the broken places of our life.

Healing Prayer

Father. Thank You for taking the broken places of my life and using them for Your kingdom. Thank you for not leaving me in my shattered state. Let your light shine through my life as never before and help me become a vessel of Your glory in Jesus' name. Amen

Healing Confession

I am God's workmanship.............................. Ephesians 2:10
I am fearfully and wonderfully made............. Psalm 149:14

Healing Action

1. Pray for the Lord to reveal any areas of your life where you feel inadequate to be used by Him, make a list in the space below.
2. Surrender any fear, insecurity, or inferiority keeping you from being who God has called you to be.
3. Ask the Lord to fill you with His confidence.
4. Search the scriptures for one that you can speak over yourself stating who you are in God that counteracts any negative mindsets.
5. Pray for The Lord to take any weak or broken areas of your life and cause them to become a light that shines for Him

God's Word for Us

And He said to me" My grace is sufficient for you, for My strength is made perfect in weakness. --- 2 Corinthians 12:9a NKJV

But God has chosen the foolish things of the world to put to shame the wise, and God has chosen the weak things of the world to put to shame the things which are mighty. --- 1 Corinthians 1:27 NKJV

For we are His workmanship, created in Christ Jesus for good works, which God prepared beforehand that we should walk in them. --- Ephesians 2:10 NKJV

Being confident of this very thing, that He who has begun a good work in you will complete it until the day of Jesus Christ. --- Philippians 1: 6 NKJV

But we have this treasure in jars of clay, to show that the surpassing power belongs to God and not to us. --- 2 Corinthians 4:7 ESV

My Thoughts Today

Day 10 - The Cry That God Hears

Psalms 107:13

> They cried out to the Lord in their trouble and He delivered them from their distress.

At some time or another, each of us will find ourselves facing the fiery trials of life, trials of affliction pain and trouble. As children of God, we understand that we can cry out to Him from our place of distress. We can trust Him to be faithful to His Word. Even when we cannot see the answers we have prayed for, we must continue to believe and trust in Him.

Several years ago, my brother and I found ourselves caring for our very ill parents. The grief of losing the Mom and Dad that we had always known became very real to us, as each day was filled with doctor's appointments, dialysis treatments, meal preparations and the need for Mom's constant supervision. The pressure of working a full-time job and caring for my parents was difficult.

I lost count of the number of times my heart desired to be free from my job so I could care for Mom and Dad the way they deserved. After months of long busy days and short sleepless nights, everything came crashing down. Weariness, hopelessness, and sorrow washed over me like a tidal wave. Thoughts of wanting our situation to end brought guilt on top of all the other emotions that were raging within me. I felt sad

69

for my Dad who was watching everything (including my Mom) slip away from him. I felt sorry for my Mom who was plagued with Alzheimer's. Most of all, I felt like a failure as a caregiver.

I am not sure how long I spent crying out to The Lord that night, spilling all that had been building up on the inside over the past months, praying in my heavenly language as tears streamed down my face.

I cannot say that I remember what changed first in our situation. I can say that something shifted within me as I prayed. The hopelessness and sorrow that I had been battling lifted. Somewhere within myself I knew that the Lord had moved. A new strength began to fill the place that had felt so weak within me. Although I was not sure just how things would change, I chose to trust God.

I saw Dad for the last time on December 31st, (about two months after my night of crying out to The Lord). Shortly after Dad passed, Mom broke her hip and had to be placed in a long-term care facility, a decision I prayed would never come. Six months and eighteen days after our Father passed, Mom took her final breath and crossed over into the reward she so deserved.

The Bible holds many accounts of those who cried out in their time of trouble, despair, and hour of need. Below are some of those accounts, the Greek and Hebrew words, and their meaning.

Quara (Hebrew), to call with a loud sound

Elijah cried out to The Lord for the widow's child who had died (1 Kings 17: 20-22), and he came back to life.

Tsaaq (Hebrew), to cry out for help

Moses cried out to The Lord when the Israelites needed water (Exodus 15:25), and God provided!

Krazo (Hebrew), to croak or cry out loud

Blind Bartimaeus cried out to be healed as Jesus walked by (Mark 10:46-52), and his sight was restored to him.

Zaaq (Hebrew), to cry or call for help

Jehoshaphat cried out to The Lord in a battle at Ramoth-Gilead and The Lord saved him 1 Kings 22:32

The results of what God did as I cried out to Him remained with me throughout the final days of caring for my parents. I am not saying there were not difficult days. I am saying that God filled me with what I needed to make it through one of the hardest seasons of my life.

God may deliver us out of our physical situation. He may free us from the spiritual battle that surrounds our circumstance. Often, He calms the battle raging within us, the emotional or mental distress which is a result of the pressure from something surrounding us. However, God chooses to work, we can trust that He will bring exactly what we need.

Healing Prayer

Father forgive me for the times I doubted You and Your Word. Forgive me for the times I cried out and did not believe that You had moved on my behalf because I could not see a change in my situation! Thank You for Your faithfulness in my life.

Healing Confession

You are my refuge and strength, a very present help in times of trouble. Psalm 46:1

Healing Action

Spend some time in worship allowing God to heal any deep and wounded places within you. Let God's love wash over you, healing and restoring the deep places of your heart and soul.

God's word for Us

The Lord is good, a stronghold in times of trouble, and He knows those who trust in Him. --Nahum 1:7 ESV

Call on Me in the day of trouble; I will deliver you, and you shall glorify Me. --- Psalm 50:15 NKJV

When the righteous cry out for help, the Lord hears and delivers them from all their troubles. --- Psalm 34:17 ESV

Then they cried to the Lord in their trouble and He delivered them from their distress. ---- Psalm 107: 28 ESV

In my distress, I called upon the Lord, and cried out to my God. He heard my voice from His temple and my cry came before Him even to His ear. ---- Psalm 18:6 NKJV

My Thoughts Today

Day 11 – Trading my Shame

Isaiah 61:7

> Instead of your shame, you shall have double honor, and instead of confusion, they shall rejoice in their portion. Therefore, in their land, they shall possess double; everlasting joy shall be theirs.

The unnamed woman who met Jesus at the well in Samaria walked away much different then she came. Everything that she had experienced in life until that moment became her testimony as she embraced the words that Jesus spoke over her.

The rest of her story (the fact that she left the well, returned to her hometown and led others back to Jesus) gives us an understanding of God's ability to put His finger on our sin, expose what is within us and transform us for His kingdom plan.

The Jews and the Samaritans of Jesus' day had a long-standing dislike for each other. Among other things the Jews believed the Samaritans mixed marriages to the Assyrians and worship of more than one god made them unclean and unworthy. The Jews' disdain toward the Samaritan people was so strong that they refused to go through their city on the way to the temple in Jerusalem. A decision that added time and effort to their journey.

This Samaritan woman, who found herself alone at the well with

Jesus, knew that nothing about her encounter would be understood by those of her day. Jews did not talk to Samaritans and men did not talk to women, especially alone. Yet here she was in the heat of the day listening to Jesus tell her everything there was to know about her life.

Shame is a painful emotion that finds its way into our life through a generational tie, an act we have taken, or an action other have taken against us. Its voice says we are defective, inferior, and unworthy. Shame operates as a false covering, working to keep us from receiving the love and forgiveness of God. It never stops saying," no matter how hard you try, you will never be enough".

Almost immediately after eating the fruit that God instructed Adam and Eve to stay away from, guilt and shame caused them to hide and cover themselves. They knew that something had changed in their lives. But they could never understand the impact that their decision would have on every generation to come.

Shame always encourages us to hide and cover ourselves. It drives us to be self- focused and over sensitive to the situations around us. Whenever possible, shame will draw us away from those who can speak truth into our life, convince us that we are better off alone and cause us to feel inferior, insecure, and unlovable.

Isaiah 61:7 tells us that our shame and confusion will be replaced with double honor and double portion. It also says that everlasting joy shall be ours.

Jesus broke through every false covering and barrier to reach the woman at the well who lived nothing less than a troubled life. Her divine encounter with Him left her with a new purpose and ability to respond to His love and acceptance.

Just as Jesus brought change to the Samaritan woman at the well, He can bring change to you. No matter how long you have been struggling to be free from shame, disgrace, or regret, The Lord wants you to know that today you can exchange all of this for his freedom and double honor.

Healing Prayer

Father, I pray today that You will remove any root of shame in my life. I surrender all shame, reproach, condemnation, and guilt to You today. Help me to see the truth of Your Word. Thank You for making a way where there seems to be no way. Amen.

Healing Confession

I trust in Your word, let me not be put to shame. — Psalm 25:2
I set my face like a flint and I will not be ashamed. — Isaiah 50:7

Healing Action

1. Shame keeps company with many other destructive emotions. Read over the list below and pray for the Lord to reveal any areas that may be affecting your life. Mark the area that you feel God is showing you.

Condemnation   Self-hatred Disgrace   Self-Pity   Guilt
Worthlessness   Fear of Failure   Unworthiness
Self-Condemnation   Inability to forgive yourself Regret

2. Pray and ask the Lord to break all ties and association between shame and the emotions that you marked.
3. Pray for the Lord to remove any generational association with shame and all other areas on your list

God's Word for Us

For the Scripture says, "Whoever believes on Him will not be put to shame. --- Romans 10:11 NKJV

For the Lord God will help Me; Therefore, I will not be disgraced; Therefore, I have set My face like a flint, And I know that I will not be ashamed. --- Isaiah 50:7 NKJV

Looking unto Jesus, the author and finisher of our faith, who for the joy that was set before Him endured the cross, despising the shame, and has sat down at the right hand of the throne of God. --- Hebrews 12:2 NKJV

Oh my God, in You I trust, let me not be put to shame, let not my enemies exalt over me. --- Psalm 25:2 ESV

My Thoughts Today

_____

_____

_____

_____

_____

_____

_____

_____

_____

_____

_____

_____

_____

_____

_____

_____

_____

Day 12 - Love Without End

Deuteronomy 7:9

Know therefore that the LORD your God, He is God, the faithful God, who keeps His covenant and His loving kindness to a thousandth generation with those who love Him and keep His commandments.

"Many things about tomorrow I don't seem to understand; but I know who holds tomorrow, and I know who holds my hand". The words to this song come to my mind almost daily. We don't know what tomorrow may bring. But whatever it may be, if we hold on to God's unchanging hand, he will see us through.

Life has a way of changing things we have planned for ourselves, our life, and our future. Everything I had hoped and prayed for from my teenage years for my family and myself would change in one day. I was raised up in a preacher's home, with God fearing parents. God has always come first in my life. I was taught to depend on him for all things, but on September 13, 1986, depending on God became a reality for me. Not by the "covering" of my parents, I had to depend on him for myself.

At 24 years of age, this was the test put before me; I was having my first child, ready for the baby of my dreams to be born and anticipating life with him going to school, college, getting married, having grandchildren, everything you hope and wish for your child. So, as I was alone, by myself, in the hospital room when the doctor came in with my baby. As I held Benjamin in my arms, he seemed so perfect, so beautiful. The doctor sat down beside my bed and told me he was almost one hundred percent sure that my baby had "Down Syndrome". At that moment, I felt all the life had been pushed out of me; I could not breathe. At that moment I was scared, but the biggest question in me was "Why, Lord?" Since a child, I had been raised in a preacher's home. All I knew was God and the church so "Why me, Lord?" At the same moment, I knew God would see me through, as He had done in times past. For some reason, He gave me this child.

I prayed that I would be able to give him back to God. I prayed for God to use Benjamin for His glory. I asked for wisdom and strength. So today at twenty-six years of age, he stands as a man of God, used greatly by Him, and for His glory. He truly hears the voice of God; he is tuned in and receptive to Gods voice in a loud, noisy, busy world. I have also grown spiritually, reading God's word, for strength and encouragement.

For I know the promises he has for me.....Jeremiah 29:11 says "for I know the thoughts that I think toward you, says the Lord, thought of peace and not of evil, to give you an expected end". God says in His Word that He will never leave me or forsake me, so as I step into each new day, knowing God is with me and will guide me for that day (one day at a time). Through Christ I can endure, cope with, manage, and complete all things.

Life has its challenges for my son, but love is the circle that he has brought into our family in more than one way. Throughout the years, love has helped us through a challenging day, It is the strong bond that only the Lord can give, God has a bond of love for every family, and we need to take it, grasp it and hold onto it. Maybe it comes to a family, as it did mine, with a child born with Down Syndrome. However, it comes to you, God has a way of bringing it to every family. Take hold of the love that God has placed in your heart; believe it can break the strong-hold of hate, fear, and bitterness we may have one for another and love each one as God has loved us as through His son, Jesus Christ

Healing Prayer

Father, forgive me for the times that I have not walked in love toward those around me. Thank you for loving me in the best and worst moments of my life. Fill me with your Holy Love. Help me to share that love with those around me. Amen.

Healing Confession

Nothing can separate me from the love of God..... Romans 8:39
He loves me with an everlasting love............ Jeremiah 31:3
I will love others as Christ has loved me........... John 13:34

Healing Action

1. Forgive those who have not shown you the Love that you have needed in your life.
2. Ask the Lord to fill your heart with a greater measure of His love
3. Choose one or two scriptures from today's scripture record them below. Work to memorize the scriptures you chose throughout the day.

God's Word for Us

Because Your steadfast love is better than life, my lips will praise You. — Psalm 63:3 ESV

And hope does not put us to shame, because God's love has been poured into our hearts through the Holy Spirit who has been given to us. — Romans 5:5 ESV

Through the Lord's great love, we are not consumed, for his compassions never fail. — Lamentations 3:22 NKJV

A new command I give to you: that you love one another. Just as I have loved you, you also are to love one another. By this all people will know that you are My disciples if you have love for one another. — John 13:34,35 ESV

Above all, keep loving one another earnestly, since love covers over a multitude of sins. — 1 Peter 4:8 ESV

My Thoughts Today

Day 13 – Disappointment, Discouragement And Hope

Luke 18:1

> Then he spoke a parable to them that men always ought to pray and not lose Heart

Discouragement, frustration, and disappointment will find their way into the life of every believer at one time or another. They work to hinder or abort the kingdom call of God, steal our hope and make us weary with their relentless attempt to distract our focus from the Lord and His assignment.

Isaiah 54:17 says that "No weapon formed against you shall prosper, and every tongue which rises against you in judgment you shall condemn. This is the heritage of the servants of the Lord, and their righteousness is from Me, says the Lord". As we shelter ourselves under the wing of our heavenly Father, and follow His Word, we will overcome every obstacle and illusion sent to work against us.

Nehemiah and the Israelites had barely begun to rebuild the wall around the old city of Jerusalem when their enemies, Sanballet and Tobiah, came with words of false accusations, ridicule, and scorn. The men's attempt to discourage the people of Judah failed leaving them in their own anger and frustration.

There were many more attempts to stop the people of Judah during the 52 days of rebuilding the wall. Each time the children of Israel were tempted to give in to the plan of their adversary, Nehemiah brought their focus back to God. He led the people with the strategy that he received from The Lord. And, in the end, Judah's enemies stood in agreement that the work they could not discourage, frustrate or stop was truly a work of God.

Discouragement and disappointment work together to separate us from our hope, courage, and confidence in God. Their goal to obstruct our advancement in the Kingdom and keep us from standing strong in the midst of adversity requires us to seek the Lord and follow his strategy.

Their ability to gain a foothold in our life can come through regrets, weariness and comparing ourselves with those around us. When we keep our focus on God, continue to work, and come together with like-minded believers, we will see victory over every attack and attempt of our enemy.

The man from the parable of the Good Samaritan, who had been beaten, robbed, and left half dead, must have dealt with many emotions as he lay alone on the side of the road. I imagine the trauma of his experience was driven deeper as the priest and the Levite each passed him by intentionally ignoring him in his wounded state.

I believe that every emotion working against this man was overcome as the Good Samaritan began to show him the love and compassion that others were unwilling to show.

Within ourselves, we might think that the Good Samaritan would have a right to be disappointed or discouraged with the priest and the Levite who refused to stop and help him. As I pondered this story, something new came to mind. The man who is referred to as the Good Samaritan might not have been the one any of us would have expected to stop and help the stranger. Yet, it was this man who had everything he needed to begin the healing process in the one he found alone on the side of the road. He had the oil, wine, and dressing for the man's physical wounds. He had a donkey that could carry the stranger to the inn where he could rest, and he had money to pay for food and shelter until the stranger was well enough to be on his own again.

We should never overlook God's divine plan and ability to bring us everything we need. It may not come through who we choose, nevertheless, if it is from God, it will meet our every need.

There are times when disappointment and frustration come to us through a stranger, as they did for the people of Judah. There are other times that it comes through those we know, love and trust. Our adversary doesn't care who he uses.

Ephesians 6:12 says that we wrestle not against flesh and blood, but against principalities, against powers, against the rulers of the darkness of this age, against spiritual hosts of wickedness in the heavenly places.

No matter how much it looks like our battle is with those around us (our family, friends, or co-workers), it is not. It is always against the forces of darkness that have the ability to twist, masquerade and deceive many.

Below are seven keys to overcome disappointment, discouragement, and frustration that we can learn from the story of Nehemiah:

Seek God first .... Nehemiah 4:4, 9

Be watchful .... Nehemiah 4:9

Don't stop working .... Nehemiah 4:6

Keep your eyes on God .... Nehemiah 4:14

Refuse to be fearful...................... Nehemiah 6:9

Reject the lies of the enemy .... Nehemiah 6:3, 4, 8

Join forces with likeminded believers .... Nehemiah 4:6, 13

The victory of The Lord is always sweeter than we could imagine and more timely than we can know. Although we may have to endure hardship as a good soldier of Christ for a season, (2 Timothy 2:3) our day of victory will come.

Healing Prayer

Father, I surrender all discouragement, disappointment, and frustration to You today. I receive Your comfort and ask You to fill my heart with courage, discernment, and wisdom. Cause me to keep my face set like flint on what You have called me to do in Your kingdom. Amen.

Healing Confession

The Lord is my healer.. (Ex 25:26)
I trust in Him .... (Proverbs 3:5, 6)
My help comes from the Lord, maker of Heaven and Earth (Ps 121: 1)

Healing Action

1. Pray to break any alignment with discouragement, disappointment, and frustration. Ask God to renew your hope and fill you with His determinations for victory.
2. Pray and ask the Lord to show you if there are any open doors to discouragement, disappointment, or frustration in your life. Make a list in the space below.
3. Spend time in confession and repentance for each item you listed. As the Holy Spirit leads, Ask the Lord to close any open doors.

Some examples opened in your life could be:

Comparing yourself with others

Inner vows (I will not let them hurt me again)

Blaming God for our struggles

Not trusting God to be our Healer, deliverer, etc.

Agreeing with fear

God's Word for Us

God is our refuge and strength, a very present help in trouble. ——
Psalm 46:1 NKJV

Then He spoke a parable to them that men always ought to pray and
not lose heart. —— Luke 18:1

But I will hope continually and will praise You yet more and more. ——
Psalm 71:14 NKJV

Why are you cast down, O my soul? And why are you disquieted within
me? Hope in God; for I shall yet praise Him, The help of my counte-
nance and my God. —— Psalm 43:5 NKJV

Be of good courage, And He shall strengthen your heart, all you who
hope in the Lord. —— Psalm 31:24 NKJV

Let us hold fast the confession of our hope without wavering, for He
who promised is faithful. —— Hebrews 10: 23 NKJV

My Thoughts Today

_____

_____

_____

_____

_____

_____

_____

_____

_____

_____

_____

_____

_____

_____

_____

_____

_____

_____

Day 14 – Peace in the Midst of the Storm

Matthew 8:26

> And He said unto them, why are ye fearful, O ye of little faith? Then He arose and rebuked the winds and the sea; and there was a great calm.

Within minutes of being asked to speak to a group of women from a local church. The Lord began to fill my heart with a message for those he would bring together. Over the next few weeks, I studied and pondered the story of the disciples who became fearful in the midst of the storm as Jesus slept in the bowels of the boat. As the wind and waves worked to overtake those on board, fear also tightened its grip.

The same followers of Jesus who had watched Him cast out demons and heal many who were sick, now had a need of their own. Jesus revealed the real issue of their heart as He spoke, "Why are you fearful, O you of little faith."

Fear, doubt, and unbelief come to steal our peace and stop our faith. As we listen to their voice over the voice of the Lord, their grip will tighten upon our life, causing our victory to seem almost impossible.

Those who were on the boat with Jesus did not struggle with doubt of who He was or of what He could do. Their battle was within themselves. It was a battle of doubt and unbelief that they could walk in the same kind of faith and authority as the one they were following.

95

As I waited to speak what I believed God had placed on my heart for the group of women, I had my own struggle as the voice of doubt spoke in my ear, "are you sure you can do this, are you certain that you are to share those words?"

I chose to trust what I believed God had placed within me; and, in that trust. I was able to watch Him in His faithfulness. Women who needed hope, faith and strength found it as the Lord blew His breath into the room.

There is an ancient custom of launching an arrow into the camp of the army that you are about to go to war with. Launching these arrows tell your opponent that you plan to overtake them in battle. Perhaps this was the thought in Elisha's mind when he ask the king of Assyria to launch his arrows out of the window.

Maybe it was to test the King's determination, or simply meant to be a prophetic act. Whatever the reason, the king, who had come to Elisha on his deathbed, failed to follow the instructions of the prophet. Elisha held nothing back with his words to the king that his failure to launch more than three arrows meant defeat. Jehoash's fear became a reality and his people became captives of the Syrian king.

There are times that we can speak to the storm of our life and the wind and waves will cease immediately, and there are times when we must speak to our storm over and over again, releasing the Word of the Lord as an arrow into the camp of our adversity until we know that our victory is complete.

God may choose to calm the storms around us. He may choose to calm the storm within us or the fear, anxiety, or the anger from the turbulence around us. More often than not, He will allow us to walk through the storms of our life using them to strengthen us, increase our faith and build His character within us.

Whatever type of storm you are facing today. God wants you to know that He is with you. He is watching over you. The God of Israel never slumbers or sleeps (Psalm 21:3). He also watches over His word to perform it in our life. (Jeremiah 1:12). The amplified version of Jeremiah 1:12 says "you have seen well, for I am (actively) watching over my word to fulfill it." Dear Friends, God actively watches and waits for us to speak His Word over our circumstances so He can fulfill it in our lives.

Healing Prayer

Father, cause Your voice to be louder in my ear than any other voice. Give me courage and fill my heart with a greater faith so I can speak to the storms of my life just as your Son spoke to the storm on the Sea of Galilee. Surround me with Your peace through every storm of my life. Amen.

Healing Confession

I confess with my mouth and believe in my heart that I can do all things through Christ who strengthens me. ---Philippians 4:13

The Spirit of Truth abides in me and teaches me all things. He guides me into all truth. --- John 16:13.

God is my peace in the midst of the storm and His faith is at work within me. --- Isaiah 26:3

Healing Action

1. Pray for The Lord to show you any fear, doubt, or unbelief at work in your life. Make a list in the space below.
2. Confess and repent of each area you listed.
3. Thank God for His forgiveness, for the work of the cross and the power of the blood of Jesus
4. Choose one or more of the scriptures from the scripture page on

faith, or find your own scripture. Write it in the space below.

5. Speak each scripture you choose out loud over your circumstance at least three times throughout the day.

God's Word for Us

Jesus said to him, "If you can believe, all things are possible to him who believes". — Mark 9:23 NKJV

Peace I leave with you, My peace I give to you; not as the world gives do I give to you. Let not your heart be troubled, neither let it be afraid. — John 14:27 NKJV

And the peace of God, which surpasses all understanding, will guard your hearts and minds through Christ Jesus. — Philippians 4:7 NKJV

My people will dwell in a peaceful habitation, in secure dwellings and in quiet resting places. — Isaiah 32:18 NKJV

You will keep him in perfect peace, whose mind is stayed on You, because he trusts in You. — Isaiah 26:3 NKJV

Great peace have those who love Your law, and nothing causes them to stumble. — Psalm 119:165 NKJV

My Thoughts Today

Day 15 – Healing Brings Freedom

Mark 8: 23, 24

> So He took the blind man by the hand and led him out of the town. And when He had spit on his eyes and put His hands on him, He asked him if he saw anything. And he looked up and said, "I see men like trees, walking."

God is Jehovah Raphe, the healer of our minds, souls (thoughts and emotions), as well as our physical bodies. Healing can be spectacular and instantaneous, or progressive over a period.

Jesus leads the blind man by the hand, out of the village of Bethsaida; he spits on the man's eyes and lays hands on him. In this account, the man can see shapes now, but his vision is still not clear or completely restored - yet!

At five years of age I was traumatized by sexual abuse at the hands of a trusted family member. My family spent a few weeks in the home of my Grandmother and her son, who lived with her, while we were relocating. For many years I suffered nightmares of a shadowy figure outlined in the doorway, with dreams of a dark crushing weight, and an evil presence that filled me with fear. Even after we moved into our own home, there were periodical visits to my Grandmother's house. After all the adults were asleep, my uncle would pay a visit to me in the middle of the night.

I spoke of what happened to me one time, but I was told never to speak of it again. So, I held the memories and their shame in my heart, locked away in secrecy, until my teenage years, when the locked door burst wide open and the repressed hurt and anguish flooded forth in a torrent of self-destruction.

My lifestyle very nearly killed me. I believe it would have if the Lord had not intervened and stepped into my life, to rescue me before it was too late. He lifted me out of the pit of despair, out of the mud and the mire. He set my feet on solid ground and steadied me as I walked along. (Psalm 40:2 NKJV).

Slowly but surely the healing began, as I was able to acknowledge the harm that was done and begin the process of forgiveness. The dreams came less frequently and power over me lessened. I thought I was completely healed until I took a closer look, through a counseling course offered at a local women's ministry. At fifty years of age, I was still afraid of the dark! It seemed a little foolish to get up in the middle of the night to open the bedroom door and turn on the hall light. So, I asked the Lord about my fear. He gently showed me the shadowy figure in the doorway and the door closing shut behind him, plunging us into the deep and dreadful darkness. Then Jesus, the light of the world, let me see that I no longer needed to fear the darkness; at last, I was completely healed, or was I?

Along with a fear of the dark, I had also suffered from claustro- phobia, which had grown in intensity over the years. I panicked when my husband and I were playfully wrestling, I walked out of elevators that became too crowed and I had to make an anxiously hurried exit from a lighthouse. Lord, where did this fear come from? Jesus, oh how I love you for showing me the frightened little girl pressed against the wall with no place to run or hide. My loving God is healing me again!

God continues to heal me in mind, soul, and body. In His healing, I have found great freedom. He brought me out into a spacious place; He rescued me because He delighted in me. (Psalm 18:19)

And so, the account of the blind man of Bethsaida ends in verse twenty-five; once more, Jesus put His hands on the man's eyes and they were opened, his sight was restored, and he saw everything clearly.

Healing Prayer

Father, Thank You, for opening my eyes so I can see more clearly. Thank You for healing the wounded places within me from my past. Shine your light upon my life. Chase away all fear and fill me with a greater faith. In Jesus' name Amen!

Healing Confession

I will always bless the Lord; His praise will continually be in my mouth. Psalm 34:1 NKJV

Healing Action

Choose 2 or 3 scriptures from today's scripture page. Write them in the space below and speak them over yourself at least three times today.

God's Word for Us

Oh, guard my soul, and deliver me! Let me not be put to shame, I take refuge in You for I put my trust in You. — Psalm 25:20 ESV

And call upon Me in the day of trouble; I will deliver you, and you shall glorify Me. — Psalm 50:15 ESV

"Do not be afraid of them, for I am with you to deliver you," declares the Lord. — Jeremiah 1:8 ESV

Stand fast therefore in the liberty by which Christ has made us free, and do not be entangled again with a yoke of bondage. — Galatians 5:1 NKJV

Behold, I will bring it health and healing; I will heal them and reveal to them the abundance of peace and truth. — Jeremiah 33:6 NKJ

My Thoughts Today

Day 16 – Deep and Secret Things

Daniel 2:22

Deep and Secret Things

> He reveals the deep and secret things: he knows what is in the darkness, and the light dwells with him.

We have an adversary who is willing to watch and wait for the right opportunity to work in our life. He will use those around us, and any circumstance available, as a tool to turn our temporary struggles into strongholds that can take years to overcome.

1 Corinthians 10:13 tell us that God will not allow us to be tempted beyond what we are able to bear and when we are tempted He will provide a way out.

Walking through the difficult seasons of our life will often leave us open for the temptation to embrace rejection, bitterness, and many other harmful emotions. When allowed to remain in our life, these destructive emotions will do their best to stow themselves away in the corner of our heart and, if possible, remain hidden for days, weeks, and sometimes years just waiting for the right circumstance that will draw them to the surface.

Not long ago, I had the privilege of helping prepare for the wedding of a close family friend. In the midst of the preparation. I found myself struggling with issues that had hidden themselves away in the corner of my own heart. Things that I believed were no longer there, but were now working their way to the surface.

As the day, progressed wounds from the past were opened; every moment seemed to bring a greater struggle. Fear of failure, rejection, insecurity and unworthiness began to speak in my ear and the voices and actions of those around me were being were used to validate every thought raging within me. I asked God "why?" "Why now?" "Why here?" Most of all, why were these issues I believed had been settled long ago, coming to the surface one more time?

How it is that God can bring us through so much that we can surrender our life to Him, and yet we find ourselves in the same struggles over and over again?

Through much prayer, constant submission to the Lord and a few tears, I made it through the day without those around seeing the internal turmoil that I was facing.

Piece by piece, over the next few weeks, The Lord allowed me to have more understanding of just how large the battle had been. The evil plan for my life was to steal my joy and use the weak areas within me, the circumstances of the day, and those close to me as a trap. God's plan was for Good! His plan was to bring a new level of freedom to my life. God knew that there was something ahead for me. He knew that I needed to be free from the bondage of my past and He knew the plan of my adversary.

I am thankful for Gods faithfulness and willingness to teach us through our struggles, and that he strives with us, always working for our good, and that he trains us in a place of His divine protection.

Even though I knew, that God had worked on my behalf, a piece of the struggle remained with me for a few weeks. Early one morning, I felt the leading of the Holy Spirit to call a trusted friend. One who was willing to speak the truth I needed to hear. Her words washed over me like a cleansing rain, "Do you need to forgive anyone"? I immediately felt a release from the torment that had been at work in my mind. As I forgave those who had unknowingly been vessels used to validate the voice of the enemy, I gained a new understanding of the parable of the unforgiving servant in Matthew chapter 18.

We may not understand how God is working but we can trust Him in the process. When we give ourselves completely to Him, He will always do what is best for us.

Healing Prayer

Father, I submit to You. I choose to trust Your plan for my life. Reveal any deep and secret thing that I need to see in my life, anything that might hinder what You have for me life in days to come. As I forgive others and surrender what has stowed away in the corner of my heart, break off any shackles and chains that are binding and restricting me. Open prison doors and break me out into the new season. Use me for Your kingdom plan and purpose. I thank You for Your perfect timing. Even when I do not understand what you are doing, I choose to trust you. Amen

Healing Confession

Do not rejoice over me my enemy, when I fall, I shall arise; when I sit in darkness, The Lord will be a light for me. — Micah 7:8

Healing Action

1. Pray for the Lord to reveal any deep and secret things within your life that need to be removed or healed.
2. Make a list and bring it before The Lord.
3. Confess and repent of actions, thoughts, or heart issues as God leads you to.
4. Surrender thoughts, plans and hurts to God.

5. Forgive anyone that God places on your heart to forgive
6. Thank God for his faithfulness to you, thank Him for outwitting the enemy on your behalf and for the new places He has for you to go.

God's Word for Us

Nothing is covered up that will not be revealed or hidden that will not be known — Luke 12:2 ESV

Whoever follows Me will not walk in darkness but will have the light of life." — John 8:12b ESV

Call to Me and I will answer you and will tell you great and hidden things that you have not known. — Jeremiah 33:3 ESV

To open their eyes, so that they may turn from darkness to light and from the power of satan to God, that they may receive forgiveness of sins and a place among those who are sanctified by faith in me. — Acts 26:18 ESV

The unfolding of Your words gives light; it imparts understanding to the simple. — Psalm 119:130 ESV

For to us, God revealed them through the Spirit; for the Spirit searches all things, even the depths of God. — 1 Corinthians 2:10 NKJV

My Thoughts Today

Day 17 – Your Scars are Beautiful

Revelation 12:11

> And they overcame him (Satan) by the blood of the lamb and the word of their testimony.

Each of us has been broken, either at the hand of others or ourselves. It is Satan's mission to bring and use this brokenness, not only to kill but to destroy.

In my own life, satan has used the abuse of my father in an attempt to destroy relationships, the ability to trust, to love and to be loved which filters down to my children, their relationships and on down through the generations after them. Like a bad wound or break left unattended infection sets in, so satan and his demons of fear, rejection, shame, anger, guilt, and anxiety set in to fester, poison and choke out any signs of life. We have a choice to remain in our brokenness or to allow God to bring healing. Only through and with him will complete healing come.

When the choice to receive healing is made, one of the first things we will learn is, the God you thought was never true was always there. He never leaves or forsakes us. The second thing we will learn is God always has a perfect plan.

The very same God who speaks in Exodus chapter three to Moses "I have surely seen the affliction of my people, and have heard their cry. I know their sorrows. I am come down to deliver them out and to bring them unto a large and good land" is the same God that speaks today! He promises us in Ecclesiastes 3:11 that he makes everything beautiful in its time and in Psalm 138:8 that He will perfect that which concerns you!

It's my understanding that once we have a broken bone and it heals the place of the break is left stronger. A wound that has healed leaves a scar; those scars tell a story. Two years ago, my niece had a baby; her protruding stomach was covered by angry red stretch marks. At that time, she thought they were so ugly. Now when she speaks of them, her face glows as she lovingly rubs her tummy as she remembers the beauty that came with her labor. Her body will always bear those marks but there is no more pain in the memory.

Such are your scars, Beautiful to God. Think of Jesus, beaten and crucified (Psalms 22). His disciples didn't recognize him after the crucifixion until he showed them his scars. (John 20: 19, 20). Jesus, the Healer who made the blind to see, the lame to walk, and gave new skin to the lepers chose to take his scars to heaven. (Revelation 5:5-9) says "And, in the midst, stood a lamb as though it had been slain. Jesus does not have to touch his scars to remember.

Picture satan the accuser of the brethren who comes to accuse. Jesus gently touches the scars in His hand, He doesn't have to speak a word but he does "they've been redeemed, I paid the price". Another time He stands gently touching His side or one of the many disfiguring marks on his body. He smiles, having a faraway look in His eyes. It's your face He sees, your scars, your victory.

Perhaps the victory hasn't come to you yet. Maybe you doubt like Thomas who needed to see and touch. In John 20: 24-29 Jesus speaks, "Because thou hast seen me thou has believed, but blessed are they who have not seen and yet believe" .Maybe you've walked in healing victory for a while and are waiting for the day you can turn those scared hands over in yours, touch them and wash them with your tears and say, "I've come through the dark:. Charles Billingsley sings a song; it can be your victory song.

I can only imagine the look in your Father's eyes

When you came back home and said.

"Look at the scars in my hands and in my side.

I just wanted you to know these are the marks of the mission.

These are the proof of all I've been through

The evidence of sin forgiven, all that I have I offer to you.

I followed the call wherever it led me.

It was worth every step of the way

I've come through the dark

bearing the marks of the mission.

It is my prayer that you have chosen victory, that you claim the promises of the Lord as your own. The promises of God make everything, including you, beautiful in time. I pray that you allow the Lord to perfect that which concerns you. That you remember healing takes time, and I pray that you never quit, that you rebuke those whispers of doubt and lies that come against you in the name of Jesus.

Stand when given the opportunity, tell your story. Let people know what your scars are. Tell about them for the glory of the Lamb who was slain from the foundation of the world who, by His shed blood, redeemed us to himself, gladly bearing the marks of the mission.

Healing Prayer

Father, forgive me for the times I doubted that you were at work on my behalf. Thank You for never leaving me or forsaking me. Bring healing to the unhealed areas of my life. Lord, turn my scars into something of beauty that others may see Your glory upon my life.

Healing Confession

I trust you Lord with all my heart, I lean not unto my own understanding, I acknowledge you Lord in all my ways that you can direct my paths Proverbs 3:5, 6

When I am weak in You, O Lord, I am strong. 2 Corinthians 12:10

Healing Action

1. Ask the Lord if there is anything in your life that may be hindering your healing (unbelief, fear, rejection etc.). Make a list of the things that come to your mind

2. Confess and surrender each area on your list to the Lord; ask Him to forgive you for allowing these things to have a part of your life as the Holy Spirit leads

3. Thank the Lord for being your healer. Thank Him for healing the unhealed hurts in your life and for making your scars into something beautiful for Him.

God's Word for Us

"For the Lord your God is He who goes with you! To fight for you against your enemies, to save you. — Deuteronomy 20:4 NKJV

For we are His workmanship, created in Christ Jesus for good works, which God prepared beforehand that we should walk in them. — Ephesians 2:10 NKJV

Yet in all these things we are more than conquerors through Him who loved us. — Romans 8:37 NKJV

Be strong and of good courage, do not fear nor be afraid of them; for the Lord your God, He is the one who goes with you. He will not leave you nor forsake you." — Deuteronomy 31:6 NKJV

God is my strength and power, and He makes my way perfect — 2 Sam 22:33 NKJV

Have you not known? Have you not heard? The everlasting God, the Lord, The Creator of the ends of the earth, neither faints nor is weary. His understanding is unsearchable. — Isaiah 40:28 NKJV

My Thoughts Today

Day 18 - Hope, a Tree of Life

Proverbs 13:12

> Hope deferred makes the heart sick: but when the desire comes, it is a tree of life.

A few years ago, I had the privileged of taking a journey to the land of Israel. As we traveled through Capernaum and stood in the valley of Megiddo, we could easily see where all the years of war and devastation have left their mark upon this chosen land. Even though many of the places we visited are only ruins of what existed in Jesus' day, they continue to make an impact on those who visit here.

Walking through the old city of Jerusalem, where Jesus ministered to the people, reminded me of the stories that are recorded in the Word of God. It also caused me to think of how God will take the places within us that look like they are in ruins and ashes, restore them, fill them with hope and give them new life. It is our heavenly Father's pleasure to heal all that needs healed and see our hope restored, just as he did for the crippled man at the Pool of Bethesda.

This man, who had come to believe that he would never find the healing he waited 38 years to see, causes me to think of hope deferred.

After many years at Bethesda, the crippled man knew about angel of the Lord who would come down and stir the water. He understood that the first one to enter the troubled water would come out whole.

What he could not fully understand was the truth that his desire to be healed mattered to God as much as it did to him.

Hope deferred can find its way into our life through many situations. A long-lasting illness, the death of a loved one, rejection, betrayal or waiting for years to see a promise of God. Whatever avenue hope deferred uses to get into our life, we can be sure that it will push us toward disappointment and discouragement.

The crippled man at Bethesda had come to believe that he was destined to a life without change. Hope deferred had filled his heart with doubt and limitation. When Jesus asked, "Do you want to be healed"? The man's reply "I have no one to put me into the water", lets us see how hope deferred can cause us to lay down our dream and embrace the lie of the enemy.

Proverbs 13:12 says that hope deferred makes the heart sick, but when the desire comes, it is a tree of life. The original Greek definition for the word sick in Proverbs 13:12 means to become weak, sick, grieved sorry or diseased. Hope deferred affects more than our mental and emotional wellbeing. It goes straight to the heart causing it to become weak, weary and full of sorrow.

Moses, Joseph, Sarah, and Abraham all met with hope deferred as they waited to reach their spiritual destination in God. After years of disappointment, questions and sometimes cynicism, they each received their dream, overcame hope deferred and saw their desire become a tree of life.

The Greek meaning of the name Bethesda is "house of mercy or house of grace, to build or rebuild". Part of its root meaning is "shame, or reproach". Every lamb sacrificed in the Temple at Jerusalem was brought into the city through the North East gate, also named the Sheep Gate. The people at Bethesda would often spend their time under one of the five porches that surrounded the pool. Five means grace in the Word of God.

Fellow believers, there is a place where the sheep of God enter, that hope deferred, shame and reproach work to get us in their grip. In this place, God will also step in, surround us with His grace and mercy, break shame and reproach off our life and fill us with hope.

Your breakthrough or healing may not come as you have imagined. It may not come through who you would think or choose. Nevertheless, with only a few words sent from the throne room of God, when your desire comes it will be a door of hope.

The water has been stirred today. Whether you need physical touch, an emotional healing or renewed vision and hope for you future, God wants to turn your desire into a tree of life.

Healing Prayer

Father, I am thankful for Your loving kindness and tender mercy. I am thankful that You never leave me or forsake me. Strengthen the weak and weary places of my heart. Restore my hope and grant me the ability to see your plans and dreams for my life. In Jesus' name, Amen

Healing Confession

Heal me, O God, and I will be healed. Save and I will be saved. Jeremiah 17:14

The Lord God is in my midst, He is mighty to save, He will rejoice over me with gladness, I will rest in His love. Zephaniah 3: 17

Healing Action

1. Pray for the Lord to renew your vision, Habakkuk 2:2.3 says "Write the vision and make it plain on tablets, that he may run who reads it. For the vision is yet for an appointed time; But at the end it will speak, and it will not lie. Though it tarries, wait for it; because it will surely come. It will not tarry".

2. Record what the Holy Spirit shows you. Keep this record somewhere so you can read it over the next few weeks as God begins to work in your life.

3. Use the word God gives you to wage a warfare against your ene-

my (read it out loud and remind him of God's plan) when he tries to fill your mind with doubt, unbelief or anything other than what God has given you.

God's Word for Us

May the God of hope fill you with all joy and peace in believing, that you may abound in Hope by the power of the Holy Spirit — Romans 15:13 NKJV

Return to the stronghold, you prisoners of hope. Even today I declare that I will restore double to you. — Zechariah 9:12 NKJV

And hope does not put us to shame, because God's love has been poured out into our hearts through the Holy Spirit, who has been given to us. — Romans 5:5 ESV

But I will hope continually and will praise You yet more and more. — Psalm 71:14 ESV

For I know the thoughts that I think toward you, says the Lord, thoughts of peace and not of evil, to give you a future and a hope. — Jeremiah 29:11 NKJV

Today's Thoughts

_____

_____

_____

_____

_____

_____

_____

_____

_____

_____

_____

_____

_____

_____

_____

_____

_____

_____

_____

Day 19 – Two Are Better Than One

Ecclesiastes 4:9.10

> Two are better than one because they have a good reward for their labor. For if they fall one will lift his companion.

Few things in life are as sweet a treasure as a true and faithful friend. One who inspires us for good, speaks the truth we need to hear and loves us, especially in those times when we have trouble loving ourselves.

An even sweeter treasure is found in a faithful friend who loves the Lord. One who knows how to stand with us in prayer and will hold us up when we are weak and weary from the battle.

Our adversary understands the importance of friendships. He also understands the power of agreement between those who love the Lord and stand in the authority of God's Word. He knows that we are more dangerous to his kingdom when we are in agreement with other faith-filled believers. He is the accuser of the brethren (Revelation 12:10) and wants us to be an accuser with him. He never stops looking for opportunities to bring strife, contention, and division into our relationships.

The devastation that betrayal brings into our life takes what was once safe and trustworthy and turns it into a place of deep hurt, and sorrow. Betrayal leaves its victim feeling stunned and rejected by the arrows that penetrate the depths of our heart. Finding its way in through jealousy, bitterness, and offence, betrayal desires to cause as much devastation as possible before moving on to its next victim.

King David experienced many victories of war in his life. At the same time, he became a casualty of a different type of war, as those he trusted allowed their heart to be filled with jealousy, bitterness, offence, and betrayal. Each time David faced betrayal, he turned to the Lord for healing and restoration from the arrows sent to destroy him. David penned the following words from Psalm 55:12-14 during one of His own experiences with betrayal: "Nor is it one who hates me who has exalted himself against me; Then I could hide from him. But it was you, a man my equal, my companion and my acquaintance. We took sweet counsel together and walked to the house of God in the throng."

Everything that began well between David and Saul changed after Saul opened his heart to jealousy, envy, and offence. The same man he once called upon to be his armor bearer, the one he trusted and depended upon to bring relief from a distressing spirit as he played his harp became the object of Saul's envy and scorn.

Not long after David refused to wear the king's armor in his battle with Goliath, something changed. Everything that had been hiding in Saul's heart came to the surface as he heard the women sing, "Saul has killed his thousand and David his ten thousand." From this moment on, Saul was overtaken and the one that he had placed so much trust in became his enemy,

David's experience with betrayal continued with his son Absalom, his trusted friend and counselor Ahithophel, and finally his wife, who scorned him for dancing before the Lord.

Betrayal finds its way into our life through those we trust. Matthew 24 tells us in the last days that many will be offended and betray one another. It goes on to say that the love of many will grow cold.

Offence is an end time strategy of our adversary. Its seeds may lay dormant for a season, but we must know that eventually they will come to the surface causing much devastation and separation in the relationships that are often ordained by God.

Recovering from betrayal takes time. Overcoming the abandonment, deep sorrow, and hurt that work to get into our heart through betrayal may take even longer. Betrayal knows no boundaries; it has no limits. Wherever it can find a way in, it will. It comes to destroy, leaving the wounded behind as it moves on to its next victim.

Today, God wants to remove any arrows of betrayal that have been sent to wound or destroy you. He wants to remove any bitterness working to take root in your life. He desires to heal every wound, whether old or new, that has come through those you once trusted.

We must remember that we wrestle not against flesh and blood but against the powers and rulers of darkness (Ephesians 6:12). Those who are used to wound us are often victims themselves. Just like us, they need the love, forgiveness, and healing of God in their life.

Healing Prayer

Father, I thank You for the gifts and the callings that You have placed upon my life. Thank You for the grace to walk in those gifts! Release me from all effects of envy, resentment, and ill will of man! Remove all arrows of bitterness, envy, and betrayal from my heart. Refresh the dry and barren places of my life. In Jesus' name I pray. Amen

Healing Confession

I will trust in the Lord with all my heart
I will lean not on my own understanding,
I will acknowledge the Lord in all His ways, and He shall direct my paths. Proverbs 3: 5, 6

Healing Action

1. Confess any unforgiveness that you may be holding onto against those who have betrayed you.
2. Pray for the Lord to forgive you as you forgive those who have hurt you! Ephesians 4: 32
3. Thank the Lord for healing the unhealed areas of your life.
4. Purpose to pray diligently for those who have been a vessel of hurt to you in your life.

God's Word for Us

It is better to take refuge in the Lord than to trust in man. --- Psalm 118; 8 ESV

Those who trust in the Lord are like Mount Zion, which cannot be shaken but endures forever. --- Psalm 125:1 NKJV

As for me, I will call upon God, and the Lord shall save me. Evening, morning and at noon, I will pray and cry aloud, and He shall hear my voice. --- Psalm 55: 16, 17 NKJV

When you pass through the waters, I will be with you; and through the rivers, they shall not overflow you. When you walk through the fire, you shall not be burned, nor shall the flame scorch you -- Isaiah 43:2 NKJV

Fear not, for I am with you; be not dismayed, for I am your God. I will strengthen you, yes, I will help you, I will uphold you with My righteous right hand. --- Isaiah 41:10 NKJV

My Thoughts Today

Day 20 - Beauty for Ashes

Isaiah 61:3

> To give them beauty for Ashes, the oil of joy for mourning, the garment for praise for the spirit of heaviness: that they may be called trees of righteousness, the planting of the Lord, that He may be glorified.

After years of carrying a name that meant sorrow, Jabez was ready for something new. The prayer that he spoke in 1 Chronicles 4 was short but mighty. It moved Jabez into a new season of his life, released God's blessings and closed the doors to his past. The five things that Jabez asked, that God would bless him, expand his territory, be with him, keep him from evil and not let him cause pain to others, were all granted. Jabez could finally be something more than the label of his mother's pain.

A new name is a powerful thing. It can mark the beginning of a new season, speak to a transition that has already happened in someone's life or give us insight into who they are becoming.

Under the old covenant, Jewish parents would often choose the name of their children by the circumstances that surrounded the baby's birth, the experience of the mother during her pregnancy, or to honor a family member.

Just before drawing her last breath of life, Rachel gave birth to her second son, a child that she had cried out and waited for. Rachel's experience with pain and sorrow led her to name her son Ben-Omi, which means son of my sorrow. The boy's father, Jacob, did not want his son to be known for the sorrow of his mother and quickly changed his name to Benjamin, which means son of the right hand.

Abraham, Sarah and Jacob all carried their given names until the Lord honored them with a new name. One that spoke to who they were called to be in His kingdom. Below is a list of each name and their meaning.

Earthy Name	Meaning	Heavenly Name	Meaning
Abram	Exalted father	Abraham	Father of Multitudes
Sarai	Princess	Sarah	Noble Woman
Jacob	Supplanted	Israel	God Prevails or heel holder

As we receive a new name in Christ, we can rest assured that something from our old nature is being replaced with a kingdom position, assignment, or character

In Jesus' day, leprosy was a life-changing disease. Those afflicted with its painful symptoms found themselves suffering social, physical and emotional consequences. The physical results of this disease left its victims scared and disfigured. On top of being banned from society, the tradition of their day required anyone with leprosy to announce their unclean state to those approaching them by calling out "I am unclean".

The one leper who returned to Jesus must have been overwhelmed

134

with his newfound healing. The words that Jesus spoke as he fell at His feet, "arise, go your way, your faith has made you well." meant many things. He would no longer be one who carried a disease that caused him to be isolated and rejected. The pain of His past could be left behind. Most of all, he was no longer known by the name that meant he was unclean. Instead, he would be called saved, healed, delivered and whole.

Many of us carry names that are not ours to carry. Isaiah 62: 2 says we shall be called by a new name, which the mouth of the Lord will name. Verse 4 goes on to say, "We shall no longer be called forsaken, nor shall your land be called desolate; but you shall be called Hephzibah, and your land Beulah; for the Lord delights in you, and you land shall be married". Those who were once known and named forsaken will become those named and known by Hephzibah, (My delight is in her).

Friends of God, whatever name you have been carrying that does not belong to you can be exchanged today for a new name. God's name, the name, you are called to be in the His kingdom

Perhaps it is time for you to trade in the name of your sickness, anxiety, doubt, or unbelief for who God has called you to be, for who He says you are! As His child, you are called healed, chosen, redeemed, and loved. You are His delight.

Healing Prayer

Father, Thank You for calling me loved, redeemed, forgiven and free. Use me for Your kingdom purpose. I pray that You would bless me, expand my territory, be with me, keep me from evil and not let me cause pain to others. Amen.

Healing Confession

I am Your workmanship.................................. Ephesians 2:10
I am fearfully and wonderfully made.............. Psalms 149:14
I am called by Your name; I am Yours.................. Isaiah 43:1

Healing Action

1. Declare that you are who God says you are
2. Thank Him for calling you loved, redeemed, forgiven. Make a list below of who God says you are. Refer to this list as needed over the days, weeks, and months of your life.
3. Speak the scriptures aloud as a declaration to your adversary when he tries to tell you that you are anything other than whom God says.

God's Word for Us

But now, thus says the Lord, who created you, O Jacob, and He who formed you, O Israel; "Fear not, for I have redeemed you; I have called you by your name; you are mine. — Isaiah 43:1 NKJV

For we are His workmanship, created in Christ Jesus for good works, which God prepared beforehand that we should walk in them. — Ephesians 2:10 NKJV

For it is God who works in you both to will and to do for His good pleasure — Philippians 2:13 ESV

Brethren, I do not count myself to have apprehended; but one thing I do, forgetting those things which are behind and reaching forward to those things which are ahead, I press toward the goal for the prize of the upward call of Christ Jesus. - Philippians 3: 13,14 NKJV

Let this mind be in you which was also in Christ Jesus — Philippians 2: 5

Behold, I will do a new thing; now it shall spring forth; shall you not know it? I will make a way in the wilderness, and rivers in the desert — Isaiah 43:19

My Thoughts Today

Day 21 – Take off Your Grave Clothes

John 11:44

> And he who had died came out bound hand and foot with graveclothes, and his face was wrapped with a cloth, Jesus said to them "Loose him and let him go."

Choosing to follow the things of the world over the truth of God's word will always result in more pain and sorrow than we could imagine.

It is this fleshly nature in all of us that works so hard to have its way in our life. Deceiving and luring us from the truth of the Lord, always seeking its own pleasure and fighting against the Spirit of the Lord within us. The more we walk in the Spirit of God, the less we will fulfill the lust of the flesh (Gal 5:16, 17).

Lazarus was in the tomb four days before Jesus made His way back to Bethany. Those who were close to him had many questions. They could not understand why Jesus had waited so long to return after Mary and Martha sent word that their brother was very ill.

They knew that Jesus loved Lazarus and his sisters. They understood His ability to touch those who were sick and make them whole. Yet they found themselves confused and bewildered by the circumstances they were facing. A settling came to many of the questions in the hearts and minds of those at the tomb as Jesus spoke "LAZARUS COME FORTH".

Within seconds of hearing these words, the man that many believed they would never see again emerged from the tomb. His hands and feet still bound until Jesus gave further instruction to loose him and let him go.

Grave clothes represent the things of our past: addictions, bitterness, depression, sickness. When we are dead, (unable to feel because of the pain or sorrow in our life), weary (from the struggles we have faced) or embracing fear, we can remain bound in our own grave clothes.

Matthew 9:16 says, "No one sews a patch of unshrunk cloth on an old garment, for the patch will pull away from the garment, making the tear worse. Covering up the issues of our life will not bring us freedom. It will cause our wound to be driven much deeper and make our addiction stronger. The only way to find true freedom, is through submitting our issue, pain, or trouble to the Lord, allow Him to remove what needs to be removed and heal what needs to be healed. He alone can bring life to an otherwise dead situation.

Jesus spoke life into Lazarus just as God blew His breath of life into Adam. There were many around who thought it was too late for Lazarus. They doubted that Jesus could raise someone who had beeOn in the grave for four days. They had forgotten the power that Jesus carried within Him. In the end, the death and resurrection of Lazarus was for the glory of God.

There will always be someone in our life ready to speak words of doubt, discouragement, and defeat. We must choose to listen to the Word of God over every other voice. We must learn to discern the voice of truth from the voice of deception and lies, and we must surrender our desires of the flesh to the will of God.

It doesn't matter how many people say it is too late, or that you will never become who you are called to be in the kingdom of God. It doesn't matter how long you have waited for God. No amount of binding that satan or you yourself have placed upon your life can stop what God has set into motion.

Today God is speaking to you to COME FORTH. Allow Him to breathe new life of His Spirit into you. He will send those who have watched and doubted to remove your grave clothes.

We are entering a day like no other in the Kingdom of God. A day of the harvest of souls it at hand. God wants to show His glory in the earthly realm like never before and He is looking for vessels willing to be houses of His glory, vessels willing to die to their flesh so He can blow the breath of His Spirit on them and through them.

Healing Prayer

Father loosen the grave clothes which have held me. Awaken Your Spirit within me. Give me strength to let go of what has held me in the past. Set me free from any words of doubt and unbelief that have been spoken over my life. Fill me with Your life and fire and quicken me to know Your will. In Jesus' name, Amen.

Healing Confession

I have been crucified with Christ; it is no longer I who live, but Christ lives in me; and the life which I now live in the flesh I live by faith in the Son of God, who loved me and gave Himself for me. Galatians 2:20 NKJV

For "'In him we live and move and have our being'; as even some of your own poets have said, "'For we are indeed also his offspring.' Acts 17:28 NKJV

Healing Action

1. Make a list of the things in your life which have become grave clothes.
2. Pray for the Lord to forgive you for the times that you trusted in people or things over Him
3. Thank Him for the freedom He has provided in your life by sending His son Jesus to the cross.

God's Word for Us

Therefore, if anyone is in Christ, he is a new creation; old things have passed away; behold, all things have become new. — 2 Corinthians 5:17 NKJV

There is therefore now no condemnation to those who are in Christ Jesus, who do not walk according to the flesh, but according to the Spirit. For the law of the Spirit of life in Christ Jesus has made me free from the law of sin and death. — Romans 8:1, 2 NKJV

And do not be conformed to this world, but be transformed by the renewing of your mind, that you may prove what is that good and acceptable and perfect will of God. — Romans 12:2 NKJV

I call heaven and earth to witness against you today, that I have set before your life and death, blessing and curse. Therefore, choose life, that you and your offspring may live. — Deuteronomy 30:19 NKJV

I say then walk in the Spirit, and you shall not fulfill the lust of the flesh. — Galatians 5:16 NKJV

My Thoughts Today

Topics

Contributors